Business & the Government: Law & Taxes

Young Adult Library of Small Business and Finance

Building a Business in the Virtual World

Business & Ethics

Business & the Government: Law and Taxes

Business Funding & Finances

Keeping Your Business Organized:
Time Management & Workflow

Managing Employees

Marketing Your Business

Starting a Business: Creating a Plan

Understanding Business Math & Budgets

What Does It Mean to Be an Entrepreneur?

Young Adult Library of Small Business and Finance

Business & the Government: Law & Taxes

Helen Thompson

Mason Crest

Mason Crest
450 Parkway Drive, Suite D
Broomall, PA 19008
www.masoncrest.com

Printed in the United States of America.

First printing
9 8 7 6 5 4 3 2 1

Series ISBN: 978-1-4222-2912-5
ISBN: 978-1-4222-2916-3
ebook ISBN: 978-1-4222-8906-8

The Library of Congress has cataloged the
hardcopy format(s) as follows:

Library of Congress Cataloging-in-Publication Data

Thompson, Helen, 1957-
  Business & the government : law & taxes / Helen Thompson.
     pages cm. – (Young adult library of small business and finance)
  Audience: Grade 7 to 8.
  ISBN 978-1-4222-2916-3 (hardcover) – ISBN 978-1-4222-2912-5 (series) –
ISBN 978-1-4222-8906-8 (ebook)
  1. Small business–Juvenile literature. 2. Small business–Law and legislation–Juvenile literature. 3. Small business–Taxation–Juvenile literature. 4. Small business–Management–Juvenile literature. I. Title.
  HD2341.T54 2014
  346.73'065–dc23
                                      2013015647

Produced by Vestal Creative Services.
www.vestalcreative.com

CONTENTS

INTRODUCTION

Brigitte Madrian, PhD

Small businesses serve a dual role in our economy. They are the bedrock of community life in the United States, providing goods and services that we rely on day in and day out. Restaurants, dry cleaners, car repair shops, plumbers, painters, landscapers, hair salons, dance studios, and veterinary clinics are only a few of the many different types of local small business that are part of our daily lives. Small businesses are also important contributors to the engines of economic growth and innovation. Many of the successful companies that we admire today started as small businesses run out of bedrooms and garages, including Microsoft, Apple, Dell, and Facebook, to name only a few. Moreover, the founders of these companies were all very young when they started their firms. Great business ideas can come from people of any age. If you have a great idea, perhaps you would like to start your own small business. If so, you may be wondering: What does it take to start a business? And how can I make my business succeed?

A successful small business rests first and foremost on a great idea—a product or service that other people or businesses want and are willing to pay for. But a good idea is not enough. Successful businesses start with a plan. A business plan defines what the business will do, who its customers will be, where the firm will be located, how the firm will market the company's product, who the firm will hire, how the business will be financed, and what, if any, are the firm's plans for future growth. If a firm needs a loan from a bank in order to start up, the bank will mostly likely want to see a written business plan. Writing a business plan helps an entrepreneur think

through all the possible road blocks that could keep a business from succeeding and can help convince a bank to make a loan to the firm.

Once a firm has the funding in place to open shop, the next challenge is to connect with the firm's potential customers. How will potential customers know that the company exists? And how will the firm convince these customers to purchase the company's product? In addition to finding customers, most successful businesses, even small ones, must also find employees. What types of employees should a firm hire? And how much should they be paid? How do you motivate employees to do their jobs well? And what do you do if employees don't get along? Managing employees is an important skill in running almost any successful small business.

Finally, firms must also understand the rules and regulations that govern how they operate their business. Some rules, like paying taxes, apply to all businesses. Other rules apply to only certain types of firms. Does the firm need a license to operate? Are there restrictions on where the firm can locate or when it can be open? What other regulations must the firm comply with?

Starting up a small business is a lot of work. But despite the hard work, most small business owners find their jobs

Business & the Government

rewarding. While many small business owners are happy to have their business stay small, some go on to grow their firms into more than they ever imagined, big companies that service customers throughout the world.

What will your small business do?

Brigitte Madrian, PhD
Aetna Professor of Public Policy and Corporate Management
Harvard Kennedy School

ONE

Why Does the Government Care About My Business?

If you're a young adult with a business, you may think having a business gives you a lot of independence. And you're right. But even then, you're not the only one involved in your business. Whether you've been running a business for a year, started it yesterday, or are just thinking about starting one, you'll have to think about everything and everyone that your business affects.

First, there are your customers. You have to give them a good product or **service**. You can't treat customers badly—you want to make their lives better with your business.

You also have to think about all the people in the business world you'll be working with. You might get some money to start

Throughout human history, people have chosen leaders and formed governments to help organize themselves and make decisions in big groups.

your business from parents or friends. You may work with other business owners to buy materials, get business advice, or start advertising.

Finally, you also will have to work with the government if you want your business to be legal. You'll be filling out forms, paying taxes, and making sure you know the law. Running a good business means a good relationship with the government—even if you're a kid!

Business & the Government

What Is the Government?

The government is the system that runs a **community**. Your town has a local government. Your state also has a government. The whole country has a government too, called the federal government.

All together, the different levels of government help your community run smoothly. Government has a lot of jobs.

A government must protect people. It protects people from harm; for example, the government makes and **enforces** laws that say hurting another person or stealing is illegal. Governments also often protect people, by protecting their freedoms to say what they want, believe what they want, and do what they want, as long as they are not hurting other people.

Governments also take care of people in other ways. They provide schools, build roads, and run parks. It also often helps people who are struggling in life, by running programs to give them food, housing, or some extra money. A lot of the time, you don't even notice the government is doing anything, because it's just a normal part of your day. Most of us don't think about the government when we're riding to school on a bus or in the car, for example. But the government made the roads, and it enforces traffic laws to keep drivers safe. It also gives money to the school you're attending and makes laws about what you learn there.

Governments do all these things using laws. In a democracy, the government has three branches, or divisions, to deal with laws. The legislative branch—a congress or parliament—makes laws. The executive branch—the president or **prime minister** and executive employees—make the laws happen. The judicial branch—judges—makes sure the laws are fair, and it gets rid of any that aren't.

DEMOCRACY AND MORE

People have used all kinds of governments throughout history. Right now, many countries practice democracy. In a democracy, the people who live in a country have a lot of say in what government does. They vote on representatives to make laws, and people have a lot of rights and freedoms. A president or prime minister is the head of the government, but her power is limited. In monarchies, which used to govern just about every country and still exist today, a king or queen has control of the government. The king or queen passes down his or her power through a family. In a dictatorship, one person (who is not a king or queen) takes power. The people of the country usually do not have much say in what goes on in the government. Some people even support anarchy, which is not having any government at all!

People don't always agree on what the government should be doing. Some people think the government should provide more services. The problem is that services and protection cost money. Not everyone wants to pay a lot for all those things. Other people think government should not interfere with people's lives as much as it does. People on both sides of these arguments, however, are part of the government. We all agree government is needed in some form or another!

Protecting Customers

The government has a role to play in business. In some countries, governments actually run businesses. In North American coun-

tries, individual business owners run businesses. The government doesn't have a huge role, but it is still involved.

One reason the government gets involved in business is to protect customers. The laws that protect customers are called consumer protection laws. Consumer is another way of saying customer—or the people who buy things from businesses. Everyone is a consumer at some point, even if he's also a business owner. Everyone buys something, at least once in a while.

The government has made a lot of laws to keep customers from getting hurt or from being unfairly treated by businesses. For example, take a look at a bottle of painkiller or a bottle of prescription medicine. By law, the company that makes the medicine has to include a list of side effects you might experience, like headaches or nausea. You can choose not to take the medicine if you think the side effects are too severe.

In a similar way, packaged food has to have nutrition labels. Nutrition labels tell you, as the consumer, what exactly is in the food you're eating. If you're trying to eat more vitamins, you'll know which foods have the vitamins you need, and how much of those vitamins they have. If you're trying to eat less sugar, you can avoid foods whose labels list a lot of sugar. Or if you're allergic to peanuts, you can stay away from foods with peanuts in them. You can make the right food choices and stay healthy because the law helps protect you. Without those laws, you wouldn't know for sure what you were eating. Businesses could put anything they wanted into the foods they sold.

Protecting Businesses

Laws aren't just about protecting customers. As a business owner, you also benefit from laws protecting business. For example,

Taxes pay for many things we may take for granted. Roads (as well as the postal service, police officers and fire departments) are paid for with taxes. These services help businesses to succeed.

Business & the Governmentes

businesses can get something called copyright protection. If you invent a product to sell, someone else could steal your idea. She might make a lot of money from your invention. The government thinks that's unfair, so you can file a patent. Then no one else can steal your idea and sell exactly the same thing. The law protects you and your business.

Maybe someday someone will want to *sue* you. Your business didn't do anything wrong, but a customer thinks you made her sick. She decides to try to sue you and get a lot of money from you. The law protects your business from having to just hand over the money. You get a chance to prove you didn't do anything wrong in a court trial. If there were no laws to protect business, you would be in big trouble.

Taxes Have a Purpose!

All the protection and services the government provides cost money. Roads, schools, police, parks, and more cost a lot of money. The government has a few ways of raising all that money. One big way is through taxes.

All people who make money or buy things have to pay taxes. They have to pay local, state, and federal taxes. In return, the government takes all the money it collects from people, and provides services with it.

Most people grumble a little when they have to pay their taxes every April. Sometimes people hate taxes so much they don't pay them. They get in a lot of trouble if the government finds out though. Not paying taxes and using government services is a lot like stealing.

Even though giving up some of the money you made during the year can be hard, you know you're helping out your

Many businesses and individuals hire experts to help them prepare their taxes each year. Larger businesses may employ tax professionals all year round.

Business & the Government

community and country. You won't be able to see exactly where your money goes. You won't know if your tax money went to repair a park or to pay a police officer. You will know that your money, added to everyone else's, is helping make the country a better place. You benefit from everything the government does with your tax money, just like everyone else does.

TYPES OF TAXES

People have to pay several different taxes, depending on how they make money and what they buy. Here are some different kinds of taxes:

- Income tax: Money that is taken as part of people's paychecks from their jobs.
- Sales tax: The extra money you must pay when you buy something. Sales taxes are usually collected by the city and the state. They vary between states, and generally range between 5 and 11 percent of each purchase.
- Property tax: People who own their own homes or land have to pay a tax on it. More expensive property equals higher taxes.

TWO

How to Organize Your Business Legally

The best business is an organized business. As your business starts to grow, you'll want to organize it legally. Sometimes you don't have to take legal steps. Is your business more like a hobby? Maybe you sell jewelry at a craft fair once a year. Maybe you trade baseball cards with friends and sell one once in a while. You don't really need to do much legally if you're just having some fun and making a little money.

As soon as your business gets more serious, though, you'll want to organize your business legally. Are you starting to advertise your business? Have you set up a website where people can buy your products? Do you want to hire an employee? Once you answer yes to these questions, now it's time to organize and figure out how to follow business laws. Your business will be more **professional**, and you'll be ready to start growing and making more money!

Licenses and Permits

Before you even start your business, you want to check to see if you need any licenses or permits. Licenses and permits are permission to do something from the government. Business owners often need them to be able to conduct business.

Part of the purpose of licenses and permits is to protect customers. As a business owner, for example, you might have to go through safety training. If you plan on selling any food, you'll need to take a food safety course and then get a permit to sell food at the end. Your new knowledge will help you keep customers safe if they buy something from your business. Because all businesses interact with other people, the government wants to make sure the businesses don't hurt anyone. The food safety course will teach you how to avoid making food that will ever make people sick.

In another example, you want to start your own hairdressing business. You like doing your friends' hair, and you think you're good enough to work with paying customers. When you start reading up on it, you realize you have to get licensed by the government. The license tells customers that you'll keep your business and hair-cutting tools clean. Your business will keep people safe.

Licenses also tell customers you know what you're doing. In fact, to get a hairdressing license, you have to graduate from a hairdressing program. You also have to pass a test. Even if you think you're already good enough to cut people's hair, you still have to go to school and get licensed. Chances are, there's still plenty you need to learn before you could start cutting hair for pay. Be sure to research licensing before you start your business. Check out the U.S. Small Business Administration website for your

Business & the Government

state's licensing rules. Otherwise, you could get in trouble with the law by running a business without the right permission.

Licenses and permits also help the government keep track of your business. Just starting up a business means you'll have to get a license from the town where you're *operating*. The government wants to know you're doing business in case you get mixed up in anything illegal. Licenses also help the government keep track of how much taxes you need to pay.

You'll need other permits for different business activities. If you want to have people come to your house to buy things from you, you'll probably need a permit. If you want to put up a sign to advertise your business, you'll also need a permit. If you plan on selling food, you'll need a permit.

Go down to city hall or your town office for the right forms. After you apply for a business license, ask if you need to get any more licenses or permits. You might as well get all the paperwork out of the way at once!

Types of Business Organization

You have a few choices about how to organize your business.

- Sole *proprietorship*: You are the only one running your business. You are personally responsible for taxes and *debts*, but you also automatically receive all the money your business makes. If your business does really well, you'll get all the money, but if you don't sell enough and go into debt, you have to pay the debt. You don't need to do anything special to call your business a proprietorship. If you're making money by selling something by yourself, you're already a sole proprietorship.

- Partnership: You run the business with another person. Partnerships are fairly simple and cheap to organize. All partners share profits and are personally responsible for paying debts and taxes. Like sole proprietorships, you might automatically already have a partnership if you're working with another person.
- Limited *liability* company (LLC): LLCs make it so you're less personally responsible for debts and business decisions. One person or several people can own LLCs. They are halfway between sole proprietorships (or partnerships) and corporations. You have to do more legal work to set up an LLC.
- Corporation: A corporation exists independently from the people who run it. The corporation is responsible for paying taxes and debts. It is more complicated to set up, but it also protects you as the owner. If the corporation can't pay its debts, you personally won't be responsible for paying them. And if the corporation gets sued for any reason, you personally won't have to go to court.

When you're just starting out, you probably want to stick to the first three choices. In fact, if you already run a small business as a hobby, you probably have an unofficial proprietorship. If you run it with another person, it's a partnership.

Incorporation

Eventually you may want to incorporate your business—turn it into a corporation. Corporations are kind of like people. Legally, a corporation can sell and buy property, sue other companies or people, and be charged for committing a crime, just like a person.

Business & the Government

Turning your business into a corporation means some extra work. You'll have to keep track of more things and write them down. You'll have to pay more taxes too. Corporations are more expensive to set up. Think carefully about incorporating your business.

Incorporation can be a really good thing and can help your company grow a lot. People incorporate for a few reasons. Sometimes they want to protect their company. Corporations can last forever, if they do good business. If you get bored running your corporation, you can pass it along to someone else. You can also pass along a corporation to a family member.

Business owners also incorporate because it can be easier to convince other people to give them money. **Investors** tend to like to give money to corporations because it's easier, and they know the company takes itself seriously. An "Inc." after your company name often makes people trust your business more.

Incorporation is also good because it protects the things you own. Let's say your business isn't doing very well, and you start to owe people money. You could get in legal trouble for not paying your debts. Then your personal money in the bank is at risk. If you happened to own a home, a car, or some land, you might have to give them up if you can't pay debts. Adults in business usually face this problem more than young people.

Some business owners eventually want to make their companies public. That means they want to divide the company into shares and sell them. Each share is a little tiny piece of ownership. By buying a share, a person shares in owning the company. Every share a public company sells makes money, which it can use to buy materials, pay employees, or do whatever it needs to do. And when a public company makes money, each shareholder (people who own shares) gets some of that money. The more

Business law can be very tricky. Luckily, it is the job of accountants and lawyers to understand these laws and translate them for you.

shares a person holds, the more money she gets. The business owners themselves usually own some shares, which is how they make money.

Get Some Help

You should get some advice before you dive into business. Lots of people have started businesses before you. Talk to some of them. Ask around at your local Chamber of Commerce, which is an

organization for businesses. Talk to business teachers at school or any business owners you know. Most people will be glad to give you advice.

Think about talking to a lawyer or an **accountant** too before you decide what to do with your business. Lawyers and accountants know all the laws, and they can help you figure out what the best choices are based on your age, your goals for your business, and how you want to pay taxes. Laws and **finances** can be hard to follow, so professionals can really help you out.

THE STOCK MARKET

The stock market is where people buy and sell shares of companies. If a company offers one hundred stocks for sale, it is offering one hundred pieces of ownership. Companies that are doing well can sell their stocks for a lot of money. Companies that aren't doing very well will sell stocks much more cheaply. In the United States, a lot of stock is bought and sold on the New York Stock Exchange. Other stock is bought and sold online, on an online market called the NASDAQ. You can be part of the stock market if you want. Research companies that have done really well for a long time, and buy their stock. If you buy stock now, and then wait years to sell your stocks, you might make a lot of money!

Real-Life Business Organization

Maddie Bradshaw is a wildly successful teenage business owner. At the age of ten, she invented a product called Snap Caps, a necklace made of bottle caps. At first, she made them just for her

You Can Start a Business, Too!

Maddie Bradshaw's

THE CREATOR OF **SNAP CAPS** SHOWS YOU HOW

by Maddie with lots of help from Mom & Margot

Starting a business as a young person is difficult, in part, because of the law. Maddie's book won't replace the advice of a lawyer, but it will help many young people interested in starting a business.

friends and family. Eventually, she took fifty of her necklaces to a local toy store. The store agreed to put them on the shelves, and within a couple hours, they were gone! In an interview, she describes her early business days by saying, "At that point, I knew I was onto something. I think we were successful in the beginning because I was more focused on having fun and less worried about failing."

Maddie knew she could make a real business out of Snap Caps. She decided to organize her business, and start making money. Maddie and her family set up M3 Girl Designs, LLC. She chose an

LLC so her mom and sister could help her run the company, and because LLCs are pretty **flexible**. The rest of her family wanted to own a little of the company. They also wanted to protect the money they had before they started the business.

Today, Maddie is very involved in M3 Girl Designs—she's the president of her company. She goes to company business meetings, advertises the company at **trade shows**, and creates new products. Her little sister is the vice president. Her mother is the CEO (the chief executive officer), which makes the business easier to run. The CEO takes care of the finances and helps make business decisions. Since Maddie is under eighteen, it's harder for her to legally run an LLC.

Maddie has learned a lot about starting and running a company. She started with $300, and now makes $1.6 million a year! She wants to teach other young people how to do the same thing, so she's written a book called *You Can Start a Business, Too*. Maddie loves business and likes to teach others about business. "I love that I have an opportunity to reach out and help others," she says.

THREE

Laws That Apply to Any Business

You're used to following laws every day. You wear your seatbelt in the car. And for that matter, you don't drive unless you're legally allowed to in your state. You go to school, which the law says you have to do. You don't steal.

When you run your own business, you need to follow some extra laws. Make sure you know what they are. Just because you don't know them doesn't mean you won't be held responsible if you break them. Figure out which business laws apply to you, and you'll be trouble free.

Advertising Laws

Advertising is how you tell other people about your business, and how you convince them to buy something from you. Unfortunately, some companies have used advertising to make false claims in the past. Now there are laws against advertising that doesn't tell the truth.

In general, your advertisements have to be truthful, fair, and must have evidence to back up what they claim. If an ad lies to get people to buy something, the business that made the ad is breaking the law and can get in trouble.

The Bureau of Consumer Protection lists the sorts of advertisements the government likes to keep an eye on.

- Ads that make claims about health or safety, such as:
  ABC Sunscreen will reduce the risk of skin cancer.
  ABC Water Filters remove harmful chemicals from tap water.
  ABC Chainsaw's safety latch reduces the risk of injury.

- Ads that make claims that consumers would have trouble **evaluating** for themselves, such as:
  ABC Refrigerators will reduce your energy costs by 25%.
  ABC Gasoline decreases engine wear.
  ABC Hairspray is safe for the ozone.

- Ads that make subjective claims or claims that consumers can judge for themselves (for example, "ABC Cola tastes great") receive less attention.

You'll want to think hard about your ads. If you're making and selling jam, for instance, you have to be careful about your ads. To sell your jam, you decide you want to make a video ad

and put it on Facebook. You really want people to buy from you. You read somewhere that vitamin C protects people from getting colds, and you know the fruit you use to make your jam has a lot of vitamin C—so your ad promises that your jam will keep people from getting colds.

In fact, you don't really have any proof to claim your jam will stop people from getting colds. You could even get in trouble for saying that. Someone might eat your jam and then get a cold. They could get angry; in a really extreme situation, they could even sue you. Or the government could find out you're making false advertising claims, and you would get in trouble.

Food product labeling is also part of advertising. Whatever you put on a product is helping sell it to customers who look at the label. Your jam labels will have to say what is in the jar, the name of your business (so customers know who made it), and how much jam is in the jar. You don't, however, need to have nutrition information on your label. Small businesses that make food don't have to put nutrition information on their products. Once you have sold a certain number of jam jars, though, you'll have to start putting nutrition information on the jars.

Every kind of business has different laws like nutrition information. Your situation will be unique. Do research to see which advertising and labeling laws your business should be following.

Environmental Regulations

Many young people who run small businesses don't have to worry too much about environmental **regulations**. A babysitting or a tutoring business doesn't affect the environment too much. Other businesses have a big **potential** to do some damage, though.

If your business works with any sort of chemicals, or if it could pollute the environment, you'll need to pay close attention to environmental regulations.

Imagine you have a lawn-care business. You use pesticides to kill bugs on lawns. You use fertilizer to keep plants and lawns healthy. The chemicals you use can pollute the ground and water, so you should be careful. You'll need to find out what the environmental laws are in your area, and if you need to have any permits to use lawn-care chemicals.

Trademarks and Patents

Certain laws help you protect the things you make. The same laws keep you from unfairly using things other businesses make. Trademarks, patents, and copyright laws all protect products and business.

Trademarks are words or symbols that identify a business. Trademarks are the names of companies, or symbols like the McDonald's arches or the Nike swoosh. Copyrights protect creative works like poems, photographs, and websites. Copyrights give the creator the right to be the only one to use her work. All books, for instance, have copyrights, which you can find on the copyright page. Patents protect inventions and products. No one else can sell a patented invention except for the person who invented it, or businesses the inventor gives his permission to.

When you create a business, you might want to protect yourself. You could use a trademark to protect your name and logo. You could copyright your website. And you could patent the brand-new thing you invented that you're selling through your business.

Anything you create is automatically copyrighted. Your new website was created by you, and no one can copy it. You might

PATENT MEDICINE

Patent medicines were mixtures of ingredients advertised as medicines in the 1800s and 1900s. People could bottle up some alcohol and vegetable juice and call it a medicine. The labels on the bottles promised miracle cures. Of course, the patent "medicines" didn't really make people less sick; they just made people drunk. Some were even dangerous and had drugs in them that are now illegal, like cocaine. Some of the more imaginative patent medicines were called Bonnore's Electro Magnetic Bathing Fluid, Dr. William's Pink Pills for Pale People, and Hamlin's Wizard Oil. Back then, there weren't any laws against false advertisements and labels. The government also didn't keep track of what medicines were being sold like it does today. After people realized that patent medicines were hurting and killing patients, the government passed laws about food and drug labeling.

want to register with the U.S. Copyright Office, though, in case someone does *plagiarize* your site. Then you can fight back legally and get whoever is using your creation to stop.

You don't automatically get a trademark or patent when you come up with a business name or logo, or a new invention. You'll have to register with the U.S. Patent and Trade Office. Many people hire lawyers before they do that, but you can also register on your own. All these laws are most useful if your business starts to grow really big, and you want to start selling to customers who aren't just in your town.

At the same time, you want to make sure you're not copying anyone else. Do your research before you start a business. If

Laws That Apply to Any Business

you want to sell something you think has never been thought of before, make sure no one else has already invented it. When you create a name for your business and set up your own website, make sure you're not copying another business's name or website design. You don't want to create a whole business and then find out someone else has already beaten you to it!

Workplace Safety

A long time ago, businesses didn't have any responsibilities to make sure the workplace was safe. In factories, people lost fingers and arms in the machines they used. In mines, people got sick from the dust or were trapped underground. Sadly, sometimes these things still happen, but now there are laws against unsafe workplaces.

You probably won't be asking your employees to do anything as unsafe as mining, but you do still have to pay attention to how safe the workplace is. Every type of business will have to deal with different workplace safety laws.

Your lawn-care business, for example, may have to follow certain laws about how employees work with chemicals. Check out the U.S. Occupational Safety and Health Administration website to see which laws apply to your specific business.

Labor Laws

Labor laws have to do with employees. When you hire people to work for you, you have to keep track of a lot of new laws. You'll only want to hire employees if your business is booming. Employees can cost you a lot of money. You have to make sure you're treating them fairly and legally.

How do you decide if you really need an employee? Think about your lawn-care business. You started out by offering to mow neighbors' lawns a couple times a week. You realize you could make a lot of money and help a lot more people. You get a business license from your town, and you start advertising your new business. You get lots of new customers. You have so many customers you never seem to have time to do your homework or hang out with friends anymore. You really care about your business, so you don't want to just give it up.

Maybe it's time for an employee. You're an official business. You need some help. And you have enough money to hire someone five hours a week. You decide an employee is the right move for your business, so you start searching. You also read up on labor laws.

A lot of employee laws are very important. By following the law, you are making *society* better. As a business owner, you can't refuse to interview or hire people based on the color of their skin, whether they're male or female, their religion, their sexual preferences, or anything else. Not only is *discrimination* illegal when it comes to hiring, it's also wrong. Everyone deserves a fair chance to work for you.

You also have to pay people the minimum wage. The minimum wage is the least you can legally pay an employee per hour. At the beginning of 2013, the federal government said the minimum wage was $7.25. States can have minimum wages that are higher, so check with your state to see what you'll need to pay your workers (at the least). And you can't make people you hire work more than forty hours a week without paying them extra.

Some labor laws have to do with employee age. Child labor laws say you can't hire young people under fourteen, with a few exceptions like babysitting and delivering newspapers. You

Laws That Apply to Any Business

Government regulations make starting a business more difficult, especially for a young person, but most regulations are there for a reason: to protect people from being exploited by their employers.

Business & the Government

ETHICS

Ethics is a system of right and wrong: how people should act. Sometimes people confuse ethics with the law, but laws can be ethical or unethical. How ethical were the laws that made slavery and discrimination legal? However, ethics and the law often overlap. Many laws are put in place because they protect people and represent the right thing to do. Children shouldn't have to spend their first years of life working, so there are laws making child labor illegal. We shouldn't pollute the environment and make drinking water and air dirty, so there are some laws against pollution.

can only employ young people who are fourteen and fifteen for a limited amount of time. People sixteen and older can be employed for any number of hours a week, except for the most dangerous jobs.

Real-Life Laws

One person who knows exactly what it's like to follow laws as a young business owner is Jason O'Neill. When he was nine, Jason started selling an invention called Pencil Bugs, which are pencil toppers. At first, he sold them at a craft fair. People loved them, so he turned his craft into a business.

Jason was nine when he started his business. Since he was a *minor*, he couldn't sign business licenses or other legal *contracts*. Only adults are legally allowed to sign them. Jason

Laws That Apply to Any Business

Jason may not have been able to legally sign business contracts, but that didn't keep him from autographing his book!

Business & the Government

says, "I think the biggest challenge was the restrictions of being a kid with a business. There were many things that I could not do legally." But he goes on to say, "My age was an advantage because people were more willing to help out and buy my products just to support me."

In another interview, Jason points out, "Being a kid and having a business can be really fun but it also means that you're probably going to need a lot of help from adults. When you're a minor, you can't sign anything legal like business licenses or contracts. . . . I'm lucky because I have my mom and dad and they help a lot." Like lots of young business owners, Jason found he needed a little help when it came to the law!

Jason has also had to deal with product safety laws. Product safety laws make sure everything sold by businesses is safe and won't hurt consumers. These laws say, for example, that all toys sold in the United States have to be tested for lead. A few years ago, the government found out that kids were getting sick from playing with toys with lead in them. Jason's Pencil Bugs counted as a toy, so he had to get them tested for lead.

First, Jason was going to send his product away to get tested. He says, "My mom and I were planning to send my products to a lady who was going to test them for lead content. [The law] requires that all products for kids twelve and under must be tested for lead content. And by everything, I mean everything; from clothes and toys to books and games. That meant it included Pencil Bugs too."

At the last moment, Jason and his mom found a company that would test his toy right in town. "We contacted them," Jason says, "and since they were within driving distance, they said we could come right away. They even invited us to stay and watch while they did the test, which was very exciting. The little lead

Laws That Apply to Any Business

PROTECTION AS AN EMPLOYEE

Not all young people want to or can own their own businesses. Plenty of teenagers get jobs to make some money and get work experience. They're someone else's employees at restaurants, stores, car washes, and more. As an employee, you have rights that protect you. You should be paid the minimum wage at your job. Your boss legally can't pay you less. You also shouldn't be scheduled to work more than forty hours a week, and if you are, you should be getting paid more than your normal wage for your overtime hours. Your workplace should be safe and healthy. You shouldn't be scared you're going to get sick or that you're being asked to do dangerous things. If you think the place where you work is breaking labor laws, tell someone! Family, teachers, and lawyers can explain the law to you and help you figure out if you should be doing something about your workplace.

testing device was so cool but much smaller than I expected. The **technician** took each part and smashed it down to as flat as she could and then put the sensor on it for a minute or so until the reading came up. After each part was tested, she recorded the numbers on a **calibration** sheet and told us the results." Pencil Bugs passed, and Jason was free to keep selling them.

Business & the Government

Laws can be hard to understand sometimes. As a business owner, Jason got to see exactly how product safety laws work. You'll have experiences like that too if you grow your own business.

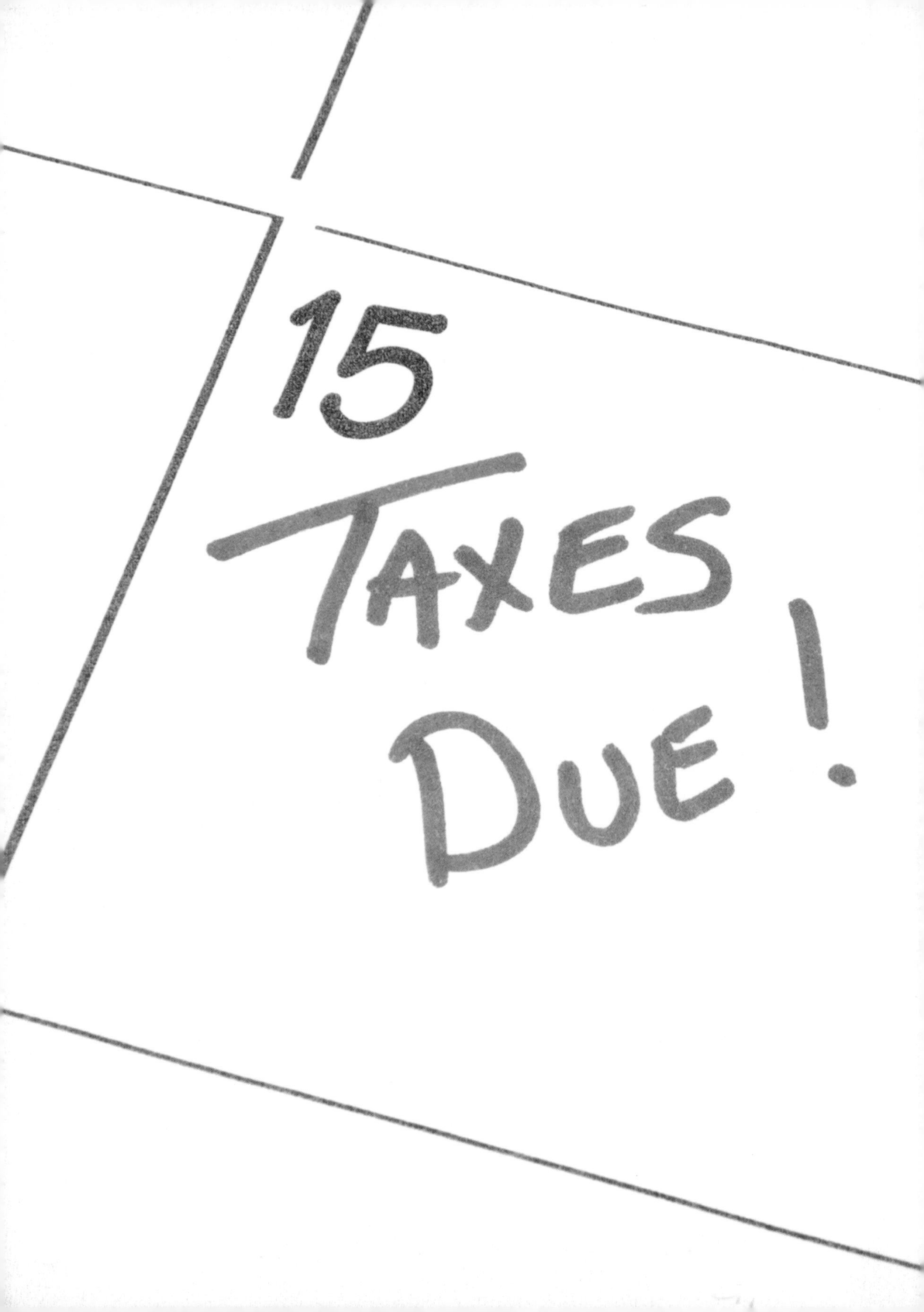
15
TAXES
DUE!

FOUR

Paying Your Business's Income Tax

Y ou might think it's unfair the government is taking away some of the money you earned. You were the one who worked so hard, so why should the government have any of your money?

Think about it a different way. Do you ever have to drive on roads or walk down sidewalks for your business? Are you getting an education at a public school, which is teaching you things you're using for your business? The government provided those things. By paying taxes, you're giving the government money to build more roads, repair sidewalks, and keep educating young people.

Famous American gangster Al Capone was eventually brought to justice on charges of tax evasion, trying to avoid paying taxes.

Business & the Government

You can choose to feel okay about paying taxes—or you can complain about them. Either way, you have to pay them. Not paying taxes is illegal and will get you into a lot of trouble. You might as well look on the bright side!

Do I Have to Pay?

Not every business owner has to pay taxes, though. Only the ones who make enough money are responsible for paying income taxes. Think of having to pay taxes as a sign your business is doing really well!

When you pay business taxes, you have to decide if you are self-employed. When you're self-employed, you make your own work; you don't work for anyone else. If you run your own business, you are self-employed. If you babysit or tutor once in a while or sell a few crafts now and then, that counts as self-employed. If you own a sole proprietorship or an LLC, you are self-employed. If you own a corporation, however, you aren't self-employed. Your corporation pays taxes separately from your own income tax.

When you're first starting out with your business, you might not need to pay income tax. Maybe you got your jam business started in July of last year. You made fifty jars of jam and sold them to your friends. Your mom took a few to work and sold them to coworkers. In all, you made $300 by January 1. You won't need to fill out tax forms and pay taxes, because your business made so little. This year, you got started earlier, and more people knew about your jam. You've already made $600 and the year isn't even over yet! You know you'll have to pay taxes this year. You won't be paying much, but as your business keeps growing, you'll need to pay a little more every year.

How to Pay

Telling the government how much you made and paying your taxes is called filing your tax return. In the United States, the deadline to file taxes is April 15. Filing after the deadline means you'll have to pay even more.

Before you even look at your taxes, make sure you have all of your money records. You need to keep track of receipts for materials you buy for your business. You should also have records of how much money you make. The best thing to do is to keep all your **expenses** and earnings on one **spreadsheet**. Good businesspeople keep their businesses organized.

You have a choice to fill out your tax forms online or on paper. Go to the Internal Revenue Service's (IRS) website to find the forms. The IRS is the part of the government that collects taxes. You'll need to figure out which forms you need to fill out.

Different kinds of companies have to file different tax forms. Go to the IRS's Small Business and Self-Employed Tax Center online to figure out which forms you will need to fill out.

Paying taxes can get really confusing. Expect to spend some time researching and doing calculations the first year you pay your taxes. You'll find paying taxes gets easier as you get used to the language of tax forms, and as you figure out which tax forms you'll need to fill out.

Pretty much every adult has paid taxes at some point, so don't be afraid to ask for help. You can even take really complicated taxes to a professional. Companies like H&R Block help people file taxes. Several companies will also help you file taxes online, like TurboTax. You'll have to pay a fee, but you'll know your taxes are right and you'll learn how to do taxes along the way.

INCOME TAX AS AN EMPLOYEE

Business owners aren't the only people who have to pay income taxes. Employees who make over a certain amount of money also have to pay income tax. In 2012, people who made more than $9,750 during the year had to pay income tax. However, dependents had to pay taxes on any income over $5,800. Dependents are people who rely on others for financial support. Young people who live at home and are taken care of by their family or other guardians are dependents. Make sure you know which category you fall into so you know if you need to pay income taxes.

Taking extra care to make sure your taxes are right is worth it. You don't want to make a mistake that catches the eye of the government. If the government sees something suspicious on your tax return, the IRS will ask you about it. You may get a letter months or even a couple years later, asking you to pay the difference between what you paid and what you needed to pay. You're better off just filing your taxes right in the first place.

State and Federal: What's the Difference?

You'll probably need to pay taxes to two different parts of the government: the federal government and your state government.

No matter what age you are, if you are doing business in America, the IRS is responsible for collecting taxes from you.

Business & the Government

The federal government runs the whole country, while your state government runs your state. Almost everyone needs to pay taxes to both governments, although there are a few states that do not have income taxes.

Every state has a few different rules about taxes. Some tax more, and some tax less. Look up your state's tax rules to make sure you know what you're doing when tax season rolls around. No matter where you live, though, you'll probably end up paying less in state income tax than federal income tax.

Income tax isn't the only tax you have to deal with as a business owner, though. If you have employees, you will also have to manage employee taxes.

State Tax

Local Tax

Social Tax

Medicare

Social Security Tax

Retirement

Medicare Tax

th Insurance

Spendi

FIVE

Managing Employee Taxes

When you decide to hire an employee, you have to do more than just interview a few people and choose the best one for the job. You also have a lot of legal stuff to do, including pay taxes.

Taxes and employee laws can get really complicated. You have to set up your business to pay taxes. You have to keep records of paychecks and taxes that have been taken out of paychecks. Once your business gets so big you need to think about these things, you should seriously think about talking to a lawyer or accountant. She'll be able to tell you exactly what you need to do, and you'll know you won't be accidentally breaking any laws. Do your own research too, so you know what's going on with your business.

BUSINESS IDEAS

Young people can start up a lot of different businesses. You don't have time to run a full-time business, so the trick is to choose something you can do when you have time after school, on the weekends, or during school vacations. Here are some ideas:

- babysitting
- pet care, including dog walking, pet sitting, and dog grooming
- crafts, including jewelry, knitting, woodworking, and more
- odd jobs (fixing things around the house)
- lawn care, including mowing lawns, raking leaves, snow shoveling, and gardening
- tutoring
- giving music lessons on an instrument or voice lessons
- blogging, which can earn money through advertisements
- selling vegetables at a farmers' market
- creating a computer game or application

Hiring Employees

Before you start hiring employees, you have to get a number from the government. The number is called an Employer Identification Number (EIN). You'll need to have an EIN to file taxes, and so you don't break the law!

Your new employees will have to fill out a couple of legal forms. One is the I-9 form, which identifies your employees as legally able to work in the country. The I-9 form is called the

54

"employment eligibility form." It is against the law to hire employees who are not legally allowed to work.

When you start hiring employees, you might also have to get something called workers' compensation **insurance**. Workers' comp, as it's known, protects employees who get hurt working for you. If one of your lawn-care employees gets hurt unloading a lawnmower from a truck and can't work, worker's comp will give him some money while he recovers.

Most states make employers get worker's compensation insurance. However, some states don't require really small businesses to have it, because it costs money. Check with your state to see whether you legally need to buy it or not.

Figuring Out Employee Taxes

As a business owner with employees, you have to pay taxes for each employee you have. Paying employee taxes can end up being a lot of money, so you have to think hard about what your business can handle before you hire an employee.

Besides the I-9, the other form new employees must fill out is called the W-4 form. W-4 forms tell you as the employer how many taxes to take out of the employee's paycheck. You'll be paying your employees every other week, or maybe monthly. Each paycheck you give them will have some taxes taken out. The taxes go to the government.

Your employee can choose to have you take a lot of taxes out of each paycheck he gets from you. Then he'll end up paying less (or even getting some money back) when he has to file taxes. He already has paid most of what he needs to give the government for the year. The employee can also choose to have fewer taxes taken out of his paychecks during the year. He'll have more

money to use during the year. But he'll also have to pay a lot of money when he files his taxes, because he hasn't paid very much yet to the government.

WHAT ARE THOSE TAXES TAKEN OUT OF MY PAYCHECK?

If you're ever hired as an employee, or if you have to pay taxes for your own employees, you'll notice there are a lot of different taxes involved. Here are the main ones:

- Social Security: this is meant to provide money to retired people. Everyone pays social security taxes when they are working. That money goes to people who are retired now (who otherwise wouldn't have a source of money). When you retire, you will receive Social Security payments from people who are paying social security then. Think of it as a savings bank for retirement, run by the government.
- Medicare: this is a health-care program for people over sixty-five and for disabled people. Medicare works a lot like Social Security, but it is specifically for healthcare.
- Unemployment tax: when employees are fired, they can get a little money to help them keep going until they find another job. The unemployment tax pays for the money that goes to unemployed workers. Businesses pay unemployment tax themselves, and don't take any money out of employees' paychecks.

Business & the Government

As an employer, you're responsible for making sure the right amounts of taxes are taken out from paychecks. You also need to pay taxes for each employee. Let's say the government takes $50 out of each paycheck you give your employee. Instead of $500, which is the amount your employee earned, she only gets $450 because of taxes. The employee pays that $50. You also have to pay some money too, because you're her employer and that's the law. You might have to pay another $50 to the government.

Owning your own business can be a great experience. You'll meet new people, learn how to be a business owner, and make some money. You'll also learn a lot about the government, because of laws and taxes. Use laws and taxes as a way to learn even more about the business world. You can't get very far in business if you don't pay attention to the government!

Managing Employee Taxes 57

Find Out More

ONLINE

Bizinate
www.bizinate.com

IRS: Understanding Taxes
apps.irs.gov/app/understandingTaxes/student/index.jsp

TeachingKidsBusiness.com
www.teachingkidsbusiness.com/
how-to-start-your-own-business.htm

U.S. Small Business Administration
www.sba.gov

IN BOOKS

Bedesky, Baron. *What Are Taxes?* New York: Crabtree Publishing, 2009.

Bernstein, Daryl. *Better Than a Lemonade Stand! Small Business Ideas for Kids*. New York: Aladdin, 2012.

Sobel, Syl. *How the U.S. Government Works*. Hauppauge, N.Y.: Barron's Educational Series, 2012.

Vocabulary

Accountant: a person whose job it is to keep money records.

Calibration: calculation, comparison with a standard number.

Community: a group of people living together in one place or sharing something else in common.

Contracts: written agreements between people that are held up by law.

Debts: money owed.

Discrimination: treating someone unfairly because of color, religion, gender, or other social identity.

Enforces: makes sure someone is following the law.

Evaluating: forming an idea about, judging.

Expenses: costs; money spent on something.

Finances: dealing with the management of money.

Flexible: able to change easily and quickly.

Insurance: coverage by contract where money is paid to an insurance company, and the company promises to pay a person if he or she experiences a specific loss (such as loss of income, health expenses, a car accident, etc., depending on the kind of insurance).

Investors: people who provide money to start or continue a business in return for sharing in the profits of that business.

Liability: responsibility for the cost of the damage.

Minor: a person under the age of eighteen.

Operating: controlling the function of.

Plagiarize: to illegally copy from someone else's work.

Potential: the possibility of being something.

Prime minister: the head of a democracy who was chosen from the legislature rather than elected directly as a president is.

59

Professional: having to do with behaviors and activities that are paid for, and thus are serious and skilled.

Proprietorship: ownership.

Regulations: rules and laws.

Service: action performed for someone.

Society: a large community of people who live together and share many values and behaviors.

Spreadsheet: A computer program used for keeping track of business numbers, in which figures are arranged in the rows and columns of a grid.

Sue: to legally ask someone or an organization for money to make up for a loss caused by that person or organization.

Technician: a person who does work using scientific tools.

Trade shows: exhibits for businesses that do similar work to share ideas and show off their products.

Index

About the Author and Consultant

Helen Thompson lives in upstate New York. She worked first as a social worker and then became a teacher as her second career.

Brigitte Madrian is the Aetna Professor of Public Policy and Corporate Management at the Harvard Kennedy School. Before coming to Harvard in 2006, she was on the faculty at the University of Pennsylvania Wharton School (2003–2006), the University of Chicago Graduate School of Business (1995–2003) and the Harvard University Economics Department (1993–1995). She is also a research associate and co-director of the Household Finance working group at the National Bureau of Economic Research. Dr. Madrian received her PhD in economics from the Massachusetts Institute of Technology and studied economics as an undergraduate at Brigham Young University. She is the recipient of the National Academy of Social Insurance Dissertation Prize (first place, 1994) and a two-time recipient of the TIAA-CREF Paul A. Samuelson Award for Scholarly Research on Lifelong Financial Security (2002 and 2011).

Picture Credits

Per RFP 03764 Follett School Solutions guarantees
hardcover bindings through SY 2024-2025
877.899.8550 or customerservice@follett.com